SYDNEY

» IN PHOTOS «

Tim Denoodle

SYDNEY

» IN PHOTOS «

EXPLORE
AUSTRALIA

ICEBERGS TAKE
NO RESPONSIBILITY
BEYOND THIS POINT

» INTRODUCTION

Sydney is where I was born and raised, and no matter where in the world I travel I always find myself returning to its bright sandstone shores. The city seems to live inside me like a painting or a poem – a vast canopy of frangipanis and Moreton Bay figs shot through with skyscrapers, surfboards and cockatoos.

Everything competes for your attention in this town: the sight of a yacht race in the wake of a ferry, the sizzle of barbecues at the local park, the squeal of kids chasing each other into the crashing surf. Wherever I go, I feel the pull of the city's saltwater fringe – the quiet harbour coves that carve to the west or the wild and playful ocean beyond the heads.

Bondi Beach is where I first experimented with a camera, and I find myself returning again and again to its famous shoreline. Even the most familiar things about this city surprise me, and building a portrait of this city with photographs has been a joyful experience. After a lifetime spent wandering these streets, there are always new things to discover and share.

TIM DENOODLE

» **LEFT** Created in the 1920s to keep local lifesavers fit during the winter months, Bondi Icebergs is home to the frigid Bondi Baths

» **PREVIOUS** Phoenix palms line the western shore of Circular Quay

» **ABOVE** Every Friday morning, a group of fluorescent-clad locals teach newcomers how to surf at South Bondi, all in support of mental health awareness

» **LEFT** From a young age, every Sydneysider is taught to swim between the flags

» **OPPOSITE** Lifesavers thread their way through a concrete field of sunbathers at Clovelly Beach

» **ABOVE** Tamarama Surf Club has strict entry rules

» **RIGHT** Heading back to the Bondi Surf Bathers' Club after an ocean swim

» **OPPOSITE** Looking South from Tamarama Surf Club on Tamarama Beach

» **ABOVE** Colourful, sandy surfboards for hire at South Bondi

» **OPPOSITE** Window view from the terrace of North Bondi Surf Lifesaving Club

» **OVERLEAF** Sails and skyscrapers compete for attention on Sydney Harbour

» **ABOVE** Catching a ferry across Sydney Harbour is the best (and cheapest) way to see the city

» **OPPOSITE** Kickboarding at North Sydney Olympic pool

» **ABOVE** No Sydney beach is complete without a flourish of lifeguard red and yellow

» **OPPOSITE** Lifeguard station at North Bondi: a staple at busy Australian beaches

>> **LEFT** Morning light at Dawes Point Park

» **ABOVE** Cafe life on Crown Street, Surry Hills

» **LEFT** Llankelly Place in Kings Cross has become a destination for all types of foodies

» **OPPOSITE** Bower Lane in Manly ends at Cabbage Tree Bay, one of Sydney's rare and beautiful aquatic reserves

» **LEFT** The golden facade of the Art Gallery of New South Wales in The Domain

»» ABOVE The striking detail of the western face of Luna Park

»ABOVE If you have enough skill, you can win big at Luna Park

» **ABOVE** Shopping with flair at the Museum of Contemporary Art

» **OPPOSITE** Established in 1891, the Strand Arcade in Pitt Street Mall is Sydney's only Victorian-era shopping arcade

» **ABOVE** William Street arts precinct in Kings Cross, where a growing number of commercial galleries and artist-run spaces have flourished

» **OPPOSITE** The Museum of Contemporary Art has been one of Sydney's premier cultural attractions since it opened in 1991

» **OVERLEAF** Looking north over the busy shores of Manly Beach

» **ABOVE** Underwater mural at Luna Park

» **OPPOSITE** Riding the gondola Ferris wheel is one of the most
popular attractions at Luna Park

» **ABOVE** Perched on the edge of the Royal Botanic Gardens, Andrew (Boy) Charlton pool is a haven for city workers who enjoy lap swimming during their lunch break

» **OPPOSITE** Testing the water during a swim session at Bondi Icebergs

» **ABOVE** The finger wharf at Walsh Bay, a destination for theatre, music and dance enthusiasts

» **LEFT** A skywriter gets creative above the Art Gallery of New South Wales

» **OPPOSITE** Despite fierce competition, Sydney Tower is still the city's tallest structure

» **ABOVE** Everyone in Bondi feels the love when it's low tide and late summer

» **LEFT** Lifeguard lookout, Bondi Beach

» **OPPOSITE** Forget yoga: stupa building has become the new way to practice mindfulness at South Bondi

» **OVERLEAF** The Domain – a stretch of open space adjoining the CBD – is popular for outdoor concerts, political gatherings and recreational sport

» **ABOVE** Puppy parking at Bondi farmers' market

» **ABOVE** Lost ball at the Bondi farmers' market

» **ABOVE** Manly Beach is prepared for all summer activities: swimming, surfing and laying out to sunbake

» **OPPOSITE** A perfect, clear summer day at Bondi Beach

» **ABOVE** Despite the suburb's gentrification, Bondi still has its throwbacks to earlier times

» **OPPOSITE** Diving into the Bronte rock pool

» **OVERLEAF** Historic Lysicrates Monument on the northern edge of the Royal Botanic Gardens

>> **ABOVE** Summer at Bondi wouldn't be the same without the hum of at least one ice cream van

>> **OPPOSITE** Waiting for customers who enjoy the soft-serve experience

>> **OVERLEAF** Sunrise and surf ski at Bronte Beach

»ABOVE Crisp white walls on Notts Avenue in South Bondi

»ABOVE Vertical gardens cover the facade of One Central Park in Chippendale

» **LEFT** Camp Cove is where the First Fleet initially moored for the night before landing further west at Sydney Cove in 1788

» **ABOVE** One More Shot Pond in Centennial Park

» **OPPOSITE** Long rows of renovated terrace houses are a familiar sight in Paddington

» **OVERLEAF** Enjoying some winter sun at Bronte rock pool

» **ABOVE** Sail rigging at The Rocks is a reminder of Sydney's maritime history

» **OPPOSITE** Hyde Park Barracks was originally built to house convict men and boys and is now a UNESCO World Heritage building

» **ABOVE** Private boats docked at Woolloomooloo's Finger Wharf

» **OPPOSITE** She-oak trees frame a view of Anzac Bridge

» **ABOVE** Iconic view out over Sydney Harbour from the rock shelf below Mrs Macquarie's Chair

» **OPPOSITE** Stark, sinuous contrasts define the Opera House

» **RIGHT** The sea wall at Bondi Beach has become famous for its mix of graffiti and contemporary art

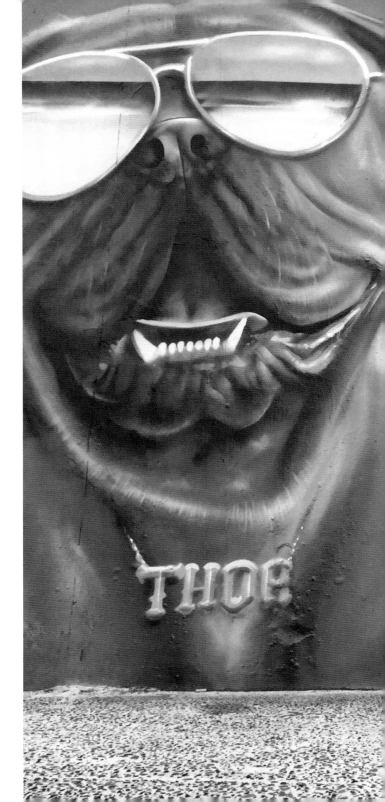

» **ABOVE** The giant chess set in Hyde Park where the public is invited to play

» **OPPOSITE** View of the quadrangle at University of Sydney in Camperdown

» **OVERLEAF** View of Tamarama Beach from Marine Drive

» **ABOVE** Wedding photos need to be finished before the storm arrives

» **OPPOSITE** Hornby Lighthouse on the South Head heritage trail

» LEFT Yoga class on the terrace of Bondi's Icebergs

» **ABOVE** Jumping off the sea wall at Clovelly Beach

» **OPPOSITE** Unrequited love on Bondi Beach promenade

» **ABOVE** Splashes of gold at Prince Alfred Park Pool

» **OPPOSITE** Cottage on the shores of Camp Cove

» RIGHT Police horses often enjoy a sandy detour in summer months at Bondi

» **RIGHT** The Manly Ferry awaits a new load of passengers at Circular Quay

» **OPPOSITE** More than a century old, the Burton Street Tabernacle in Darlinghurst became Eternity Playhouse in 2013

» **OVERLEAF** Checking out the swell at North Bondi

» **RIGHT** Cooling off with an ice-cream at Bondi's famous kite festival, Festival of the Winds

» **OPPOSITE** The Australian and Aboriginal flags always fly in unison at Bondi Icebergs

» **LEFT** One of several boats docked at Ben Buckler Amateur Fisherman's Club in Bondi

» **ABOVE** Paper lanterns decorate a Bronte Beach picnic hut

» **OPPOSITE** Sun shining on the underbelly of the Harbour Bridge

» **ABOVE** Mirrored sculptures at Darling Harbour reflect their surroundings

» **LEFT** Built in 1902 as a control cabin for a bridge across Cockle Bay, this building is now part of a pedestrian walkway

» **ABOVE** Summer skate moves at South Bondi

» **LEFT** Street art next to the Powerhouse Museum in Ultimo

» **OPPOSITE** Narrabeen rock pool is a favourite for swimmers on Sydney's northern beaches

» **ABOVE** Netting covers a peach tree in Manly to protect the fruit from local birds

» **LEFT** Looking skyward through a grove of paperbark trees in Centennial Park

» **OPPOSITE** Willow trees hang gracefully over the Chinese Garden of Friendship at Darling Harbour

»ABOVE Taking a leap into Clovelly Bay

» **ABOVE** Located in the heart of The Rocks, the King George V Recreation Centre is popular with city workers

» **ABOVE** Completed in 1934, the Hyde Park War Memorial consists of an Art Deco ziggurat in red granite

» **OPPOSITE** The ever-changing shapes of the city skyline

»LEFT Some days you swim at your own risk at Bondi Icebergs

» **ABOVE** Soft light falls through the interior of St Mary's Cathedral

» **OPPOSITE** Quiet reflections in the forecourt of St Mary's Cathedral

» **ABOVE** Flower shop in Darlinghurst

» **RIGHT** When your outfit matches the magnolias that are on sale

>> ABOVE Poppies on Macleay Street, Potts Point

107

» **ABOVE** Dawn light on a superyacht moored at Campbell's Cove Jetty, with Sydney Opera House behind

» **LEFT** Harry Sidler-designed MLC Centre in Martin Place

» RIGHT The El Alamein Fountain on Darlinghurst Road has been a Kings Cross landmark since its construction in 1961

» **LEFT** Carriageworks in Redfern has been transformed from disused railyard into one of Sydney's most vibrant creative hubs

» **RIGHT** Sydney Tower gets squeezed by the buildings on Market Street

» **ABOVE** Readying the kayak for a morning paddle

» **OPPOSITE** Steps leading down to Collaroy Beach

» **LEFT** Detail of Macquarie Lighthouse at Vaucluse, Australia's oldest and longest serving lighthouse

» **ABOVE** Located on the edge of the Royal Botanic Gardens, Japanese artist Kimio Tsuchiya has created a network of stranded Sydney stones

» **OPPOSITE** The walk from Mosman Bay Wharf to Cremorne Point is one of Sydney's best-kept secrets

» **ABOVE** The imposing columns of the State Library of New South Wales in Macquarie Street

» **OPPOSITE** Atop the Archibald Fountain the figure of Apollo reaches towards the spires of St Mary's Cathedral, Hyde Park

» **LEFT** A member of North Bondi Surf Lifesaving Club looks out from the club's rooftop terrace

» **LEFT** Ornamental trees at the Chinese Garden of Friendship

» **OPPOSITE** St Mary's Cathedral as seen from Hyde Park

» LEFT A kayaker makes his way across Blackwattle Bay towards the Sydney Fish Market

» **ABOVE** Concrete factory on the Glebe foreshore

» **OPPOSITE** Taking a break between skate moves in Bondi

» **ABOVE** The Sydney Gay and Lesbian Mardi Gras parade crosses the halfway point at Taylor Square

» **RIGHT** The smoke and confetti of Mardi Gras fly over Oxford Street

» **OPPOSITE** Admiring the view down William Street before the start of the City to Surf fun run

» **ABOVE** Low tide at Bondi makes for a perfect football field

» **ABOVE** Lifeguards pack away their sun shelter after a weekend of keeping the beach safe

» **ABOVE** When the surf is flat, there's always refuge at the Bondi skate park

» **OPPOSITE** Dee Why rock pool has been constructed around existing sandstone
to enhance its charm

» **ABOVE** Backyard oasis on the Bondi to Bronte coastal walk

» **OPPOSITE** The famous Jed's Foodstore in the back streets of North Bondi

» **LEFT** Police horses receive some early morning training in Centennial Park

» ABOVE Busbys Pond in Centennial Park

>> **ABOVE** The undercarriage of the Harbour Bridge viewed from its southern pylon

>> **LEFT** Morning run around Mrs Macquarie's Chair

» **ABOVE** Terrace houses on Lower Fort Street curve around The Rocks

» **OPPOSITE** Australia's first governor, Captain Arthur Phillip, immortalised in the Royal Botanic Gardens

» RIGHT Contemplating the ocean from Bronte Marine Drive

Published in 2018 by Hardie Grant Travel, a division of
Hardie Grant Publishing

Hardie Grant Travel (Melbourne)
Building 1, 658 Church Street
Richmond, Victoria 3121

Hardie Grant Travel (Sydney)
Level 7, 45 Jones Street
Ultimo, NSW 2007

hardiegranttravel.com

Explore Australia is an imprint of Hardie Grant Travel

A Cataloguing-in-Publication entry is available from
the catalogue of the National Library of Australia at
www.nla.gov.au

Sydney in Photos
ISBN 9781741175455

Commissioning editor
Melissa Kayser

Project editor
Kate J. Armstrong

Editorial assistant
Aimee Barrett

Design
Erika Budiman

Typesetting
Megan Ellis

Prepress
Megan Ellis and Splitting Image Colour Studio

Printed in China by 1010 Printing International Limited

» **COVER AT TOP & BACK COVER** Detail of the million-plus ceramic tiles
that form a stark chevron pattern across the Sydney Opera
House's shells

» **COVER AT BOTTOM** A crowded summer day at Bondi Beach, Sydney's
most iconic foreshore